SCAR

Compiled by Julia Skinner

With particular reference to the work of Dennis Needham

THE FRANCIS FRITH COLLECTION

www.francisfrith.com

Based on a book first published in the United Kingdom in 2006 by The Francis Frith Collection®

This edition published exclusively for Identity Books in 2010 ISBN 978-1-84589-411-5

British Library Cataloguing in Publication Data

Did You Know? Scarborough - A Miscellany
Compiled by Julia Skinner
With particular reference to the work of Dennis Needham

The Francis Frith Collection
Frith's Barn, Teffont,
Salisbury, Wiltshire SP3 5QP
Tel: +44 (0) 1722 716 376
Email: info@francisfrith.co.uk
www.francisfrith.com

Printed and bound in Malaysia

Front Cover: **SCARBOROUGH, ST NICHOLAS CLIFF 1890** 23476Ap

The colour-tinting is for illustrative purposes only, and is not intended to be historically accurate

CONTENTS

INTRODUCTION

Scarborough has been called 'the Queen of English watering-places'. Spread out like an amphitheatre upon a bay and promontory, its houses rise tier beyond tier away from the sea. The extensive remains of 12th-century Scarborough Castle crown the headland. Scarborough was the first town on the dramatic coast of Yorkshire to exploit the commercial possibilities of a seaside holiday, although in the early days it attracted the gentry for health reasons rather than pleasure seekers from the urban West Riding.

In the early days Scarborough had been developed as a spa town; the therapeutic qualities of its waters were first discovered in the 1620s. The earliest building over the spa was little more than a wooden shelter built for the convenience of people wishing to drink the waters. It was claimed that drinking the water of a small stream which flowed across the beach on what is now Foreshore Road would cleanse the stomach and blood, and would be a cure for asthma, jaundice, leprosy, melancholy, scurvy and other ills. Disaster struck in 1737 when a landslip destroyed the spa, and it was two years before it was able to be reopened. By this time the spa was housed in a pump-room, but this too was destroyed and replaced in 1839. Scarborough was now a major tourist attraction for the genteeler classes; this was reflected in the new spa buildings, which by the late 1850s included a concert hall. Scarborough continued to maintain its genteel airs and graces, and objected to the coming of the railways on the grounds that it wanted nothing to do with the great unwashed: 'the watering place has no wish for a greater influx of vagrants and those who have no money to spend'. Be that as it may, Scarborough did become popular with working people, though for a number of years it managed to maintain two distinct seasons - a fashionable and a popular one.

As well as being a holiday resort, Scarborough also had a busy harbour in the past. In the days when herring were still plentiful, Scarborough would be a calling point for the hundreds of drifters that followed 'the silver darlings' on their migration south. The oldest part of the harbour is still almost exclusively the preserve of working boats. It is sad that the days of assorted cargo boats discharging on the quay along Sandside are no more. Scandinavian timber boats were once regular visitors, but the small port was unable to handle the size of vessels increasingly in use today. Yachts and cruisers can be found in the new section to the east.

Scarborough is still a busy holiday resort, but has had to adapt to the needs of the modern holidaymaker. Thousands of visitors each year enjoy the entertainments, the attractions and the stunning location of the resort, but it is also a pleasant place in which to live and work. It is said that Scarborough once visited is never forgotten, and the town continues to be the jewel on Yorkshire's coast.

The story of Scarborough is full of fascinating characters and events, of which this book can only provide a brief glimpse.

THE SANDS AND THE HARBOUR 1890 23461

YORKSHIRE DIALECT WORDS AND PHRASES

'Mebbe' - maybe, perhaps.

'Beck' - a stream.

'Ginnel' - an alleyway between houses.

'Gang' - to go.

'Gradely' - good, as in 'It were reet gradely' - It was really good.

'Growler' - pork pie.

'Goodies' - sweets.

'Keks' - trousers.

'Lake' or *'laik'* - to play, or skive off work, as in *'Is he laiking agin?'*.

'Lop' - a flea.

'Mytherin' - to worry about something, or as in a child being annoying - *'Stop mythering me!'*.

'Sen' - self, as in *'Get thee-sen on'* - Go away.

'A bunch a'fives' - a fist, or a punch.

'Allus at't last push up' - always at the last moment.

'Brass-necked' - very confident.

'If tha' dances wi' devil, tha' ge't pricked wi'-is 'orn' - If you dance with the devil you'll get pricked by his horns, ie you will suffer if you do evil deeds.

'I'll go t'foot of our stairs!' - I'm very surprised!

'Think on' - Think about it.

'It caps owt' - It beats everything.

The Yorkshire version of the *'See No Evil'* saying:

Hear all, see all, say nowt.
Eat all, drink all, pay nowt,
And if thy ever does owt for nowt,
Allus do it for thee-sen.

HAUNTED SCARBOROUGH

There are many tales of ghosts, ghouls and witches associated with Scarborough, and one of the best ways to find out about them is to join one of the organised Scarborough Ghost Tours which are run throughout the year. Here are a few of the stories:

In 1312 Edward II's favourite and possible lover, Piers Gaveston, was captured at Scarborough Castle and taken to Warwick Castle where he was held prisoner and then executed despite being assured that he would be allowed safe passage to London. It is said that the headless spirit of Gaveston returns to Scarborough Castle to haunt the ruins, and that he sometimes lures people over the edge of the castle to fall down the cliffs to their deaths. Some visitors have reported feeling a strange sensation, as of a pushing hand, accompanied by the sound of laughter.

The steps of Church Stairs Street are associated with the ghost of Jane Nicholson, who legend says was a Scarborough witch and possibly also a vampire.

There have been reports of mysterious occurrences at the Clifton Hotel. Voices of people arguing have been heard coming from an empty bedroom on the first floor, and on the second floor on some occasions, usually after the rooms have all been cleaned and closed up ready for new guests. The doors of all the bedrooms have also sometimes been found wide open, with the television sets in the rooms switched on and playing loudly for no obvious reason.

The old Three Mariners' Inn in Scarborough was once used as a temporary morgue for bodies of sailors drowned in shipwrecks and found washed up on the beach. At one time the inn was said to be haunted by a ghost in the shape of a headless woman, who appeared to sailors staying in the inn as a warning not to go to sea when bad weather was expected. Any sailor who saw the phantom but ignored the warning was sure to be drowned.

SCARBOROUGH MISCELLANY

A Roman signal station, built cAD370, formerly stood on the site of Scarborough's castle. It was one of five such stations which formed a chain along this stretch of the coast from Redcar to Flamborough Head. From these stations a watch was kept for raiders from the North Sea, and if any were sighted warning beacon fires would be lit to warn garrisons further inland.

Evidence of early settlement dating from between 700BC and 400BC has been discovered in the Scarborough area, but the town is believed to have been established by Norsemen around AD966. Tradition says that two Norse brothers, Kormak and Thorgil, were marauding along the coast when the latter decided to settle in the area. Thorgil was nicknamed 'Skarthi' ('hare-lip') and so the name of the settlement became 'Skarthi's burg' ('Skarthi's stronghold'), which later became Scarborough.

The settlement at Scarborough was destroyed in 1066 by the army of Harald III of Norway and his ally Tostig Godwinson, the brother of King Harold of England. The Norwegian forces were defeated soon after at the battle of Stamford Bridge by King Harold, who then marched his forces down to Sussex in record time and was killed at the Battle of Hastings a few days later.

In 1381 Scarborough was attacked by the Scottish forces of Robert Bruce, along with Northallerton, Boroughbridge, and Skipton, and the town was burnt to the ground.

Bathing machines are seen
lined up on the beach in
photograph 39460, above,
overlooked by the imposing
bulk of the 365-bed Grand
Hotel. Ladies wishing to
bathe would enter the
machines from the landward
side and horses would draw

the contraptions down into the water. Meanwhile, the ladies were
donning their bathing apparel inside, and would emerge through
the door and slip, dignity intact, into the shallows. Whilst they were
bathing, the horses would be harnessed to the other end of the
machines for the return journey. Scarborough is often claimed to
have been the first resort on the north-east coast to introduce
bathing machines on to its beach. There is a written record of them
being hired out by three ladies in 1797.

The magnificent Spa buildings at Scarborough were originally built to a design by Sir Joseph Paxton. Unfortunately these did not survive a fire in 1876, and the whole area was rebuilt (shown in photograph 23450, below). This complex lasted for almost a century, then extensive refurbishment took place, which managed to retain the essentially Victorian opulence of the building whilst providing the facilities expected today. An example of this opulence was seen when the 1st Earl Londesborough, who was immensely rich and had a villa in The Crescent, invited his friend the Prince of Wales to make three royal visits to Scarborough between 1869 and 1871: a mile of red carpet was laid out to allow the Prince to walk from The Crescent to the Spa.

THE SPA SALOON 1890 23450

In photograph 23465, opposite, we see boats from a variety of ports, including Hull and Penzance. SH412 is a Scarborough yawl, a type primarily employed on lining or drift net fishing for herring, though some were converted for trawling. Yawls varied in length from about 45ft to 60ft, were ketch-rigged and sported elegant lute sterns. The ability to remain at sea for several days meant that the yawls could exploit less crowded areas of the North Sea beyond the busy herring grounds.

The Census returns for Scarborough over two centuries make interesting reading. For instance, the population of the town in 1801 was 32,947; by 1901 it had risen to 73,519, and by 2001 the population was 106,233. In 1851, 137 in every 1,000 live births died in their first year; by 1911 this figure had reduced to 102 in every 1,000, and in 2001 the figure had gone right down to 6 in every 1,000.

SOUTH CLIFF 1897 39453

FROM THE FISH PIER 1890 23465

The visitor centre of Scarborough Castle is housed in what was formerly the Master Gunner's House. This was originally built to store gunpowder, but in 1740 the building was converted into a home for the chief gunner of the castle garrison. Similar buildings can be seen at the castles of Dover, Chester, and Walmer, but they are much smaller than that at Scarborough. The Master Gunner's House was derelict and used as a rubbish dump for many years, but English Heritage has now restored the building.

The headland around Scarborough is home to an important colony of kittiwakes, small gulls which are now becoming quite rare. The numbers of kittiwakes have been in decline in recent years, for reasons which are not fully understood. South Bay is also visited by grey seals and the occasional dolphin, and whales and basking sharks (the second largest fish in the sea, but quite harmless) have also been spotted there in the past.

FISHING BOATS 1890 23467

Photograph 23467, above, shows the crews of several Lowestoft-registered trawlers taking advantage of low water to carry out maintenance on the hulls of their vessels. Note that the capstan fires are kept lit. This seems to have developed into a tradition with Lowestoft skippers so that they could set sail immediately upon leaving a port. It was standard practice on these boats to run the sheets and halyards through the steam capstan, enabling the capstan operator (usually the skipper) to handle the sails by himself.

The Queen's Tower of Scarborough Castle is named after Richard III's wife, Queen Anne, who stayed in the castle in 1484.

St Martin's Church, off the Esplanade, has several wonderful examples of Pre-Raphaelite art. These include a chancel roof by William Morris and Philip Webb, and glass and murals by Sir Edward Burne-Jones, Dante Gabriel Rosetti and Ford Madox Brown.

In the 19th century an attempt was made to develop the holiday trade with the construction of a chain pier in North Bay (see photograph 28822, below). Finished in 1869, it cost £16,000 to build, but the location was quite suspect: the way that the sea beats the Marine Drive area should have provided the builders with a warning. On the stormy night of 8 January 1905 the waves battered the elegant ironwork into submission, and the North Pier was no more.

NORTH BAY FROM THE CASTLE 1891 28822

There are some ancient buildings close to the harbour - Quay Street has one that dates back to 1300. Opposite the old harbour in Sandside is Richard III House, where the king is reputed to have stayed in 1483; the medieval building was refaced in Elizabethan times.

Probably the most famous prisoner to be kept in Scarborough Castle was George Fox. He was the founder of the Society of Friends (the Quakers), and was incarcerated for seventeen months in the 1660s in unhealthy conditions in the now-ruined Charles's Tower.

Scarborough Castle had an eventful Civil War. In 1642 Sir Hugh Cholmley was sent to hold the castle, the town and its port for Parliament, but in 1643 he and all but twenty of his men changed sides and declared for the king. This meant that Scarborough now became the prime Royalist port in the north of England. The castle was recaptured for Parliament in a night attack by 40 seamen led by Captain Browne Bushell, Cholmley's cousin, whilst Sir Hugh was away at a meeting with the king at York, but Captain Bushell was persuaded to return the castle to Sir Hugh on his return. Scarborough then remained a strong Royalist base until January 1645, when the town came under attack from Parliamentary forces. The Royalist forces abandoned the town and port and retreated into the castle. The castle was then besieged and heavily bombarded from land and sea until those inside were forced to surrender on 25 July, having run out of food and gunpowder; the defenders had also been hit by illness, and at the time of surrender only 25 men were still fit for duty.

THE SPA PROMENADE
1890 23452

15

THE LIGHTHOUSE 1890 23470

The lighthouse shown in photograph 23470, above, was built on Vincent's Pier in 1810, but it was destroyed during the First World War, on 16 December 1914 (see page 25). A replacement was erected in 1931.

After the Civil War siege of 1645 Scarborough's castle was repaired and placed in the command of Colonel Boynton, with a garrison of 100 men and 60 gunners, to defend the port of Scarborough for Parliament. Unfortunately the men were not paid, and when the second phase of the Civil War broke out in July 1648 Boynton and his men changed sides and declared for the king. Loyal Parliamentarian forces were sent to besiege the castle for a second time, and Boynton surrendered in December.

There are few recorded references to the fishing village of Scarborough before the Civil War, but we know that in 1225 Henry III granted 40 royal oaks to be used in the building of a harbour, and that in 1251 he also granted a charter to the bailiffs and burgesses 'and other good men of Scardeburgh' which stated 'it is for the benefit of the Town of Scardeburgh to make a certain new port with timber and stone towards the sea whereby all ships arriving thither may enter and sail out without danger as well at the beginning of Flood as at High water'.

The lake in Peasholm Park is the scene sometimes in the summer for a series of naval warfare battles staged by manned miniature battleships, complete with pyrotechnics.

PEASHOLM PARK c1955 S71140

SOUTH BAY 1897 39333

VINCENT'S PIER 1890 23471

In 1312 Thomas, Earl of Lancaster, uncle of Edward II, and a group of allies declared war on the king, angered by his dependence on his favourite, Piers Gaveston, rather than experienced lords. Gaveston was charged by the king to defend Scarborough Castle and did so with great courage, refusing to surrender. When food ran out, Gaveston was forced to yield, and was promised safe conduct to London. However, when he emerged he was seized and taken to Warwick, where he was summarily executed shortly afterwards, an event which shocked many people even in those brutal times. This event may be the basis for the phrase 'A Scarborough warning', which means that no warning at all is given.

In St Sepulchre Street is the Hospital of Trinity House. This was founded in 1602 to provide a refuge for retired sailors, and was one of only four such refuges in the country, all of which were along the east coast - the others were at London, Hull and Newcastle. There were no formal pension arrangements in those days, and sailors would contribute to the running of the houses during their working lives, so that they had somewhere to live when they became too old to go to sea.

Scarborough is famous for its fair, commemorated in a well-known folk-song. Scarborough Fair was first permitted in a royal charter of 1253, and in the Middle Ages it was a trading festival which lasted for six weeks and attracted merchants from all over Europe, the Baltic and even the Ottoman Empire. It ran from Assumption Day, 15 August, until Michaelmas Day, 29 September. The Fair continued to be held until the late 18th century.

THE CASTLE c1955 S71093

Scarborough Castle dates back to 1160, but the site on the promontory has been in use for much longer: there is evidence that Bronze Age and Iron Age people lived here, and the remains of a Roman signal post are still visible within the walls of the castle. The stronghold once stood 100ft tall, with walls 12ft thick; the keep was positioned in such a way as to command the approach to the causeway leading to the castle. Any attacking force attempting to enter the bailey would have to run the gauntlet of defending fire from the keep's battlements. Scarborough endured two determined sieges during the Civil War, in 1645 (see page 14) and 1648; on both occasions starvation forced the Royalist garrison to surrender to the Parliamentarian forces, and after the second siege the castle was partly destroyed to prevent it being of further military use. The castle was still being used by volunteer artillery units for gun drills and firing practice in the 19th century. Only the ruins of the keep and the barbican now remain, but they sometimes echo to the sound of musket and cannon when the Sealed Knot stage re-enactments of the 1648 Civil War siege.

A visitor writing a letter in 1733 described the bathing at Scarborough:

'It is the custom for not only gentlemen, but the ladies also, to bathe in the seas; the gentlemen go out a little way to sea in boats (called here 'cobbles') and jump in naked directly: 'tis usual for gentlemen to hire one of these boats and put out a little way to sea a-fishing. The ladies have the conveniency of gowns and guides. There are two little houses on the shore, to retire for dressing in. What virtues our physicians ascribe to cold baths in general are much more effectual by the additional weight of salt in sea-water: an advantage which no Spaw in England can boast of but Scarborough'.

The song 'Scarborough Fair' was made famous in the 1960s by Simon and Garfunkel. Paul Simon learnt the song from the English folk-singer Martin Carthy, but the tune and some lines from Carthy's arrangement had also been used a few years earlier by Bob Dylan, disguised as 'Girl From the North Country', on his album 'The Freewheelin' Bob Dylan'.

In 1381, 500 rebels at Scarborough took part in the Peasants' Revolt after swearing oaths to 'the Commons of England'. For most of them, as in the rest of the country, the revolt offered a chance to pay back old scores in their local area, and in Scarborough John Stockwith, the collector of the hated poll tax, was seized, robbed and imprisoned. Some of the bailiffs of the town fled, whilst others were taken prisoner and forced to sign ransom notes. After the disturbances were over, the ringleaders were fined, and peace was restored.

Henry VIII's religious changes of the 16th century were highly unpopular in the north of England, leading to a rebellion known as the Pilgrimage of Grace of 1536. During this uprising Scarborough Castle was besieged by the rebels, and was badly damaged by their cannons. The garrison held fast under the command of Sir Ralph Eure, who was later granted the guardianship of the castle for life, as a reward for his loyalty to the king. The Pilgrimage of Grace was put down savagely; many of those involved were executed including one of the leaders, John Wyvill, who was hung in chains outside Scarborough.

FORESHORE ROAD 1890 23464

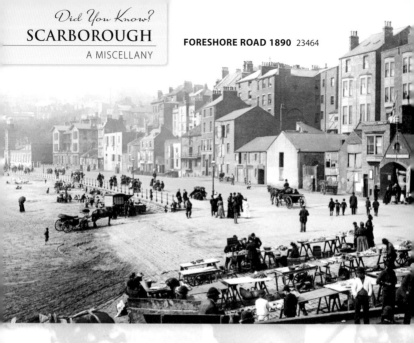

Photograph 23464, above, shows a market in the foreground where people could buy fresh fish straight off the local boats. On the right of the photograph is the old lifeboat station. The lifeboat was slung on a wheeled cradle which would be hauled out of the station, down the ramp immediately in front of it, and into the sea; the boat floated off once there was sufficient water under her. As traffic on the road increased it was decided to re-locate somewhere more convenient. The old station was sold in the early 1960s to the Jaconellis, local ice cream makers. They paid £11,000 for it, took down the old building and replaced it with something more appropriate to their trade. The story is still told of how old Mrs Jaconelli, signing a cheque for what was then a substantial sum, could not understand how an old shed could be worth so much. The new lifeboat house can be seen in photograph S71148 on page 38. Scarborough lifeboat station has so far been responsible for saving around 900 lives.

The film 'Little Voice' starring Jane Horrocks, Michael Caine and Brenda Blethyn was filmed on location in Scarborough and the surrounding area.

On 16 December 1914, during the First World War, two German cruisers took up station off Scarborough and fired over 500 shells into the defenceless town. A number of people were killed and much damage was done to the curtain wall of the castle, as well as the Royal Hotel, the Grand Hotel and other buildings. This action soon spawned a slogan for the enlistment posters all over the country that urged young men to join up and fight the enemy. It ran: 'Remember Scarborough? Enlist Now!'

NORTH BAY c1955 S71071

To the north of Peasholm, the caravan sites begin. Before caravanning became such a popular pastime, there were large holiday camps of chalets (which were built with asbestos walls) to cater for the visitor on a budget (see photograph S71067 below). These small buildings with spartan facilities provided an

inexpensive holiday for many people for whom staying in a hotel or boarding house was beyond their financial reach. Along with the huge Butlin's complex at nearby Filey, these manifestations of the 20th century are now only a memory.

HOLIDAY CHALETS c1955 S71067

The Rotunda Museum was built in 1828 to a design suggested by William Smith, sometimes called 'the Father of English Geology', who had come to Scarborough after his release from debtors' prison. He had been attracted by the geological richness of the coastline of the area, and is famous for his pioneering work which showed that geological strata could be identified and dated by examination of the fossils contained within them. The Rotunda Museum was one of the first purpose-built museums in the country, and when it opened in 1829 the display featured a collection of geological rocks and fossils which illustrated Smith's theories. Smith designed the museum to show exhibits arranged in layers from the floor to the ceiling, which illustrated the geological periods in a visual way; visitors who wanted to inspect the exhibits more closely could do so on a wheeled platform. In the 19th century fossil hunting and the study of geology became popular interests and many visitors came to Scarborough, drawn both by the interesting geology of the area and by its association with William Smith. The Rotunda Museum has undergone a major refurbishment and reopened in 2008 as a museum of geology that commemorates William Smith's contribution to Scarborough.

In 1301, Edward I asked Scarborough to provide two warships to help fight the Scots off Berwick-on-Tweed, showing that Scarborough already had a shipbuilding industry by that date. Shipbuilding continued to be significant in Scarborough for hundreds of years, and by the beginning of the 19th century this was one of the most important shipbuilding centres in the country. 209 ships were built here in the period between 1785 and 1810 alone. Ship repairing could also be undertaken in Scarborough after a floating dock capable of taking ships up to 300 tons was constructed in the mid 19th century.

In the town centre, opposite the train station, is the former cinema that was reopened as Scarborough's Stephen Joseph Theatre. Here, the famous English playwright Alan Ayckbourne premieres his new productions. Alan is a long-time resident of the town, and has also been the artistic director of the Stephen Joseph Theatre for over 50 years. His concept of theatre is to do away with a stage and proscenium arch, and to seat the audience around a central area where the action takes place, a concept known as 'theatre-in-the-round'; this technique was quite revolutionary when it was first used in Scarborough, in a play directed by Stephen Joseph which was staged in a room over the town library in the 1950s. This production at the first 'theatre-in-the-round' venue in the United Kingdom is commemorated by a blue plaque at the library.

Scarborough was a centre of the smuggling trade in the past, and one of the more colourful 'free-traders' was George 'Snooker' Fagg, who was active in the 1770s in his heavily-armed schooner, the 'Kent', which had 16 four-pounder guns. The local revenue cruisers were wary of engaging this powerful ship, and to some extent George Fagg was allowed to continue his unlawful trade. On one occasion in 1777 Fagg even made fun of the revenue men by inviting several of them on board the 'Kent' and sending them back to their own vessel with a free half-anker of smuggled gin, after hearing that their own provisions on board ship were low. Smuggling has been romanticised in folklore, fiction and film, but was actually a vicious and violent trade, full of intimidation and corruption in high places, and there are several stories about Scarborough smugglers which show its more unpleasant side.

THE PIERHEAD 1890 23472

Photograph 23459, above, shows the South Cliff tramway. This offered holidaymakers an alternative means of escape from the beach to the Esplanade, other than by the 224 steps cutting through the Spa Gardens, and all for just one penny. This was the first of its kind to be built in Britain, and opened in 1875. It is operated by a counter-balanced cable-hauled hydraulic system.

The last king to stay in Scarborough Castle was Richard III, who was there in 1484 mustering a fleet whilst he awaited the expected invasion of Henry Tudor, later Henry VII. He had been given Scarborough's castle, the lordship, the Crown rents and the port in 1473, whilst he was the Duke of Gloucester, and made the port of Scarborough the supply base for his war ships.

Scarborough Castle was seized by Thomas Stafford in April 1557, during the reign of the unpopular Queen Mary. Stafford proclaimed himself Protector of the Realm and unsuccessfully tried to raise support for his rebellion against the queen; a few days later the castle was taken by the Earls of Westmorland and Shrewsbury and Stafford was captured and sent to London for his execution. Stafford's supporters in Scarborough were executed locally, but in a particularly barbaric way - they were killed, boiled and their skins tanned in public in the town.

The Parliamentarian force besieging Scarborough Castle in 1645 during the Civil War was commanded by Sir John Meldrum, who fell off a cliff during the process of setting up the cannons around the castle after his hat was blown off by a gust of wind. He survived the fall but took six weeks to recover, only to die later in the siege when he was shot. The Royalist governor of Scarborough Castle during the Civil War, Sir Hugh Cholmley, described its bombardment and siege in 1645 by Parliamentarian forces under Sir John Meldrum in his memoirs: 'Meldrum ... hee falls over the cliff amonst the rockes and stones att least steeple height ....Yet hee is taken up for dead, lyes 3 dayes speachless, his head opened and the bruised blood taken out ... [he] recovered this soe perfectlie that with in six weekes hee is on foote againe, and beginns to batter the Castle .... soe furiously that in 3 dayes the great Tower splitt in two, and that side which was battered falls to the ground, the other standing firme beeing supported by an arch of stone that went through the midst ....The fall of the Tower had disloged the Governor, his Ladie, and most of the gentlemen and officers of qualitie, whoe were forced to betake themselves to poore Cabbins reared against the walls and banckes in the Castle yard.'

FROM THE FISH PIER 1890 23466

THE VIEW FROM NORTH CLIFF c1955 S71091

By the end of the 18th century Scarborough had a very busy port: in 1787, 1,500 seamen were recorded as belonging to the port of Scarborough, of whom 500 sailed in the East India Service. In 1796, 165 ships were registered at the port, with a total tonnage of 25,600 tons. The goods exported from the port included corn, butter, hams, bacon and salt fish, while coal, timber, hemp (for rope-making), flax, iron, brandy and wine came into the country through Scarborough.

The event that really turned Scarborough into a successful holiday resort was the coming of the railway. The self-styled Railway King - George Hudson - was the first to drive the iron road into the town, and Scarborough and York were linked by rail on 7 July 1845. Subsequently, a line south to Filey, Bridlington and Kingston-upon-Hull would be built. An even more scenic route saw trains leave to the north for Whitby, Redcar and Middlesbrough. This was a dramatic route, disconcertingly close to the cliffs at times, which made for a sensational journey; the line closed in 1958, although some of the track bed is still available to walkers. In the second half of the 19th century, cheap travel and some limited time allowed off work had introduced seaside holidays to the working class. Scarborough became a magnet for the workers from the industrialised areas of the West Riding. Guest-houses flourished, and a whole range of attractions were developed to keep these new visitors entertained. As much of the town is built on a plateau overlooking the two bays, and to allow easy access from the town to the beach, three cliff railways were built on the south bay; these operate to this day, although a further one which used to operate on the north side of the bay is now closed (seen in the foreground of photograph S71091, opposite).

THE BAY 1886 18240

The theme of the song 'Scarborough Fair' is a series of impossible tasks set by a young man to his unfaithful lover; he tells the listener to pass on the message that he will take her back if she can knit him a shirt without a seam, then wash it in a dry well, and so on - a poetical way of saying that it is unlikely that they will ever be reconciled. The song has a refrain of 'Parsley, sage, rosemary and thyme' which is full of folklore symbolism appropriate to the theme. Parsley was supposed to take away bitterness; sage symbolises strength; rosemary represents fidelity, love and remembrance (rosemary was sometimes worn in the bride's hair at weddings); and thyme symbolises courage and steadfastness.

Dame Edith Sitwell, famous for her poetry and other literary works, was born in Scarborough in 1887 - her family had a summer home at Wood End, which is now the town's Natural History Museum. Edith was an unusual sight: she stood 6ft tall, and often dressed in an unusual manner in gowns of brocade or velvet and wore a gold turban and a plethora of rings. Her best-known work is perhaps 'Still Falls the Rain', a poem about the London blitz, which was also set to music by Benjamin Britten. Edith had two younger brothers, Osbert and Sacheverell Sitwell, who were also well-known literary figures in their own right, and originals of Edith's work and that of Sir Osbert are on display at the Wood End Museum. Noel Coward once wrote a skit about Edith Sitwell and her two brothers, calling them 'The Swiss Family Whittlebot'.

SOUTH BAY c1960 S71103

THE BEACH c1955 S71145

THE BEACH c1955 S71148

The author and traveller Daniel Defoe described Scarborough thus in the 1720s: 'Scarborough next presents it self, a place formerly famous for the strong castle, situate on a rock, as it were hanging over the sea, but now demolish'd, being ruined in the last wars. The town is well built, populous and pleasant, and we found a great deal of good company here drinking the waters, who came not only from all the north of England, but even from Scotland. It is hard to describe the taste of the waters; they are apparently ting'd with a collection of mineral salts, as of vitriol, allom, iron, and perhaps sulphur, and taste evidently of the allom. Here is such a plenty of all sorts of fish, that I have hardly seen the like, and, in particular, here we saw turbets of three quarters of a hundred weight, and yet their flesh eat exceeding fine when taken new'.

South Bay is dominated by the imposing Grand Hotel, which was opened in 1867. It has 365 bedrooms, 52 chimneys, 12 floors and 4 turrets, representing the days, weeks, months and seasons of the year. When it was first built it was the biggest brick building in Europe. In later years the Grand Hotel was used as a Butlin's Holiday Centre; Butlin's sold the hotel in 1998, but it is still open today under the ownership of Britannia Hotels.

In medieval times Scarborough residents had to pay a Gablage Tax on 15 August, the opening day of Scarborough Fair. The amount paid depended on the orientation of the house - people living in houses with the gable facing the street had to pay 4 pence in the 13th and 14th centuries, whilst those whose house fronts faced the street had to pay 6 pence. The tax dated from 1181, and constituted the first form of rates, or Council Tax, to be levied in the town!

CASTLE HILL 1890 23469

In 1980, during an archaeological excavation on Scarborough Castle's headland, a Bronze Age sword was found. The sword is about 3,000 years old, and is particularly interesting as it was found almost perfectly preserved, not broken into fragments for ritual purposes, as most such finds have appeared to be. Before the important find could be put on public display it had to be sent to the British Museum for inspection, and somehow it ended up being stored away in the basement there for 25 years, forgotten by almost everyone. However, in 2005 the sword was tracked down and returned to Scarborough, where it can now be seen at the visitor centre at Scarborough Castle.

Peasholm Park was built on what was once Northstead Manor. The stewardship of this place is held to be an 'office of profit under the Crown'. Along with the better-known Chiltern Hundreds, being granted stewardship is the only way a sitting MP can leave Parliament. Holding such an office, the MP is automatically banned from sitting in the House.

SPORTING SCARBOROUGH

The Scarborough Amateur Rowing Club was founded in May 1869, and is the oldest surviving rowing club on the north-east coast. For more than 100 years sea rowing has taken place on the Yorkshire coast between the Tees and the Humber; the tradition began with friendly rivalry between the fishermen and the jet miners from Blyth, and the sport has progressed to what it is today. Rowing takes place throughout the summer months.

Scarborough's finest sporting venue is surely the Scarborough Cricket Ground. Yorkshire have played here almost every year since 1878. The ground hosted one day international cricket in the 1970s, and has always been very popular with spectators. In 1947, a record crowd of 22,946 attended a game against Derbyshire.

Scarborough Cricket Festival used to be held in September, but is now held in July. There are usually challenge matches involving overseas players (and occasionally the current touring side), and a County and Sunday League game to make up the programme.

Scarborough Football Club can claim to be one of the oldest in the country, having been founded as far back as 1879, nine years before the founding of the Football League. Perhaps the finest era in the club's history was the mid 1970s, when the club won the prestigious FA Trophy at Wembley on three occasions. Another notable highlight came in 1987. 'Boro became the first club to be automatically promoted to the Football League, when they won the newly founded Vauxhall Conference League.

Scarborough FC were pioneers in stadium-naming sponsorship. In 1988 the club sold naming rights for its stadium to McCain, the food manufacturer. Since then the ground has always been known as the McCain stadium. This was the first time naming rights had been sold in this way in England.

Bill Nicholson is probably the most high-profile sporting figure to come from the town. Nicholson was born in Scarborough in 1919. He joined Tottenham Hotspur at the age of 17, and spent over 60 years at the club, and is certainly the single most important individual in the club's history. As manager he led them to the League and Cup 'double', the first team to do this in the 20th century. His team also won the first European trophy won by any English club, the 1963 Cup Winners' Cup.

QUIZ QUESTIONS

Answers on page 48.

1. Scarborough is on the shore of the North Sea - but by what name was the North Sea previously known?

2. Which of the famous literary Brontë sisters is associated with Scarborough?

3. Charles, Henry and Oscar - what is the Scarborough link between these names?

4. Why was the Holbeck Hotel in Scarborough in the national news in 1993?

5. What is the connection between Scarborough and the 'Titanic'?

6. Which Scarborough-born writer said 'My personal hobbies are reading, listening to music, and silence'?

7. Scarborough often features in which popular television series?

8. If you are a 'Coronation Street' fan, who might you see in Scarborough?

9. Scarborough originally developed as a spa where people came to drink the waters, but is there any real benefit to drinking the Scarborough mineral water?

10. How did Scarborough's role in the Civil War make people in London shiver?

HOLIDAYMAKERS c1955 S71056

RECIPE

SCARBOROUGH MUFFINS
Muffins are rather like crumpets, but can also be used like toast, topped with a fried egg etc for breakfast.

Ingredients

350g/12oz plain flour
300ml/½ pint milk
1 egg

A pinch of salt
15g/½oz fresh yeast, or ½ tablespoonful dried yeast

Warm the milk and stir in the yeast. Beat the egg and add to the milk. Mix the salt into the flour, and work into the milk, making a stiff dough. Roll out lightly and cut into round cakes. Let them rise in a warm place for 30 minutes, than bake on a baking sheet for 30 minutes in a hot oven - 230 degrees C/450 degrees F/Gas Mark 8; turn the muffins halfway through cooking. Serve hot, cut in half and spread with butter.

THE FISH MARKET c1955 S71131

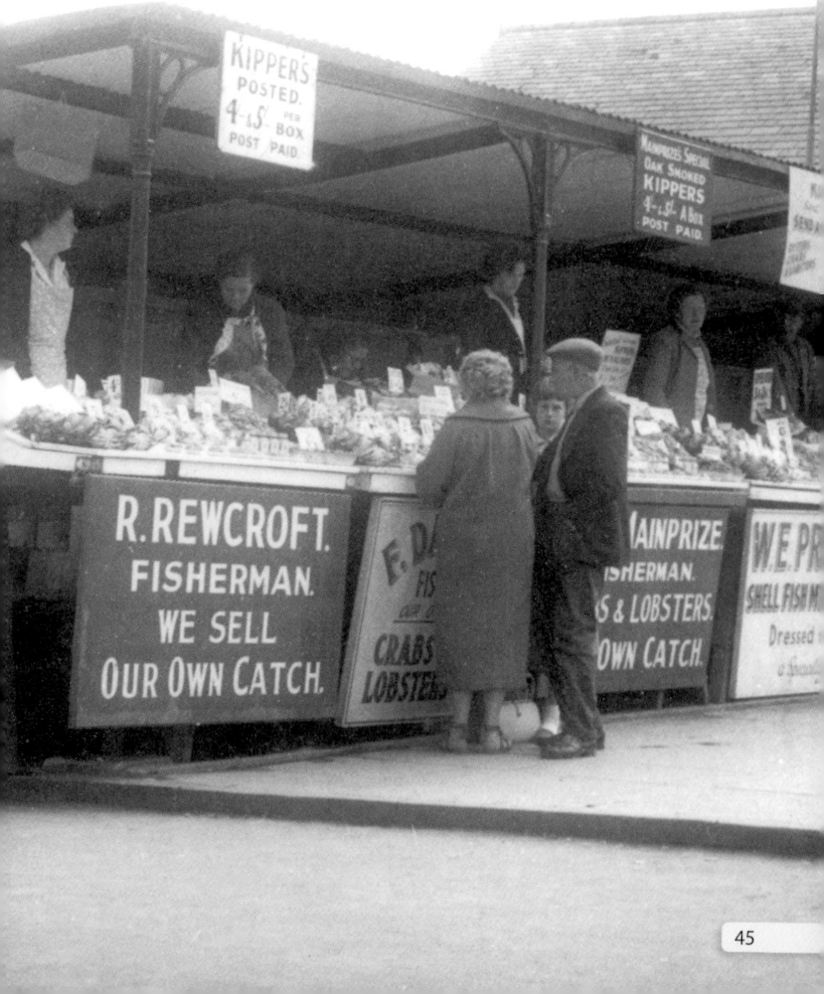

CASTLE DOCKS 1890 23468

RECIPE

SUMMER PUDDING

This was a popular pudding with visitors to hydropathic establishments in spa towns such as Scarborough because it was lighter than pastry-based puddings, which were thought to be heavy and indigestible. For this reason it was sometimes known as Hydropathic Pudding.

Ingredients

10 slices of crustless white bread - use bread from a proper loaf, not a sliced and wrapped one, for best results
3 tablespoonfuls of milk

100g/4oz caster sugar
750g/1½lb soft fruit - use a variety of such fruits as raspberries, cherries, redcurrants, blackcurrants, white currants, loganberries or strawberries

Reserve a few pieces of fresh fruit to decorate. Lightly butter a pudding basin of 1litre/1¾ pint capacity. Moisten the bread with milk. Hull, stone or top and tail the fruit as necessary. Cook it all very gently in the sugar in a saucepan over a low heat for 4-5 minutes until the sugar melts and the juices run. Spoon off a few spoonfuls of the juice as it cools and reserve. Line the sides and bottom of the pudding basin with the bread slices, cutting them to fit where necessary and checking that there are no spaces. Reserve enough bread slices for a lid. Pour in the fruit, which should come almost to the top, and cover closely with the remaining bread. Put a small plate over the top (it should just fit inside the rim of the basin), and weight it with something heavy. Leave to press overnight in the fridge.

To serve, remove the weight and the plate. Place a deep serving dish over the top of the pudding basin and reverse quickly so that the pudding comes out easily in one piece. Pour the remaining juices slowly all over the pudding, especially over the places where the juice has not seeped through the bread slices thoroughly. Keep cold until ready to serve, then decorate with a few pieces of fruit and serve with cream.

QUIZ ANSWERS

1. The North Sea was formerly known as the German Sea, or German Ocean.

2. Anne Brontë, the youngest of the famous Brontë sisters, loved Scarborough and visited many times; she used the town as the background to her novel 'Agnes Grey'. She died from tuberculosis in Scarborough in 1849 whilst on holiday in the town with her sister Charlotte. She was buried in the churchyard of St Mary's, and her grave is visited by hundreds of people every year. The Grand Hotel was later built on the site of the house where she died, No 2 The Cliffe.

3. Scarborough was the birthplace of the actor and film star Charles Laughton, whose parents were hoteliers in the town. Born in 1899, his first theatrical performance as an amateur was in 1923; by 1932 he had won an Oscar for his performance as the king in the film 'The Private Life of Henry VIII'. He also became well known for his part as the autocratic father, Mr Barrett, in 'The Barretts of Wimpole Street'.

4. Scarborough made the headlines in 1993 when the clifftop Holbeck Hotel literally fell into the sea as erosion caused its foundations to give way.

5. Shipbuilding was once carried on in Scarborough. One of the last yards to close was Tindalls. An employee of Tindalls at the time of closure was Edward Harland; in 1858 he moved to Belfast and continued shipbuilding there. Two years later he teamed up with Gustav William Wolff, thus creating the famous company of Harland & Wolff which was responsible for the construction of many fine trans-Atlantic liners and warships, including the 'Titanic'.

6. Dame Edith Sitwell, born in Scarborough in 1887, whose family had a summer home at what is now Wood End Museum (and see more information on page 37).

7. The old town of Scarborough often features in the ITV series 'The Royal'.

8. Liz Dawn, who plays Vera in 'Coronation Street', and Malcolm Hebden, who plays Norris, both have holiday homes in Scarborough.

9. The mineral waters of Scarborough have been analysed and found to contain a high content of magnesium sulphate. This means that the healing properties of the water are certainly as effective as Andrews Liver Salts.

10. For some time during the Civil War, Scarborough was a Royalist stronghold. Its port was a base from which ships in the North Sea were intercepted, particularly those carrying coal from the Newcastle area. This helped to cause a serious coal shortage in London.

FRANCIS FRITH

PIONEER VICTORIAN PHOTOGRAPHER

Francis Frith, founder of the world-famous photographic archive, was a complex and multi-talented man. A devout Quaker and a highly successful Victorian businessman, he was philosophical by nature and pioneering in outlook. By 1855 he had already established a wholesale grocery business in Liverpool, and sold it for the astonishing sum of £200,000, which is the equivalent today of over £15,000,000. Now in his thirties, and captivated by the new science of photography, Frith set out on a series of pioneering journeys up the Nile and to the Near East.

INTRIGUE AND EXPLORATION

He was the first photographer to venture beyond the sixth cataract of the Nile. Africa was still the mysterious 'Dark Continent', and Stanley and Livingstone's historic meeting was a decade into the future. The conditions for picture taking confound belief. He laboured for hours in his wicker dark-room in the sweltering heat of the desert, while the volatile chemicals fizzed dangerously in their trays. Back in London he exhibited his photographs and was 'rapturously cheered' by members of the Royal Society. His reputation as a photographer was made overnight.

VENTURE OF A LIFE-TIME

By the 1870s the railways had threaded their way across the country, and Bank Holidays and half-day Saturdays had been made obligatory by Act of Parliament. All of a sudden the working man and his family were able to enjoy days out, take holidays, and see a little more of the world.

With typical business acumen, Francis Frith foresaw that these new tourists would enjoy having souvenirs to commemorate their days out. For the next thirty years he travelled the country by train and by pony and trap, producing fine photographs of seaside resorts and beauty spots that were keenly bought by millions of Victorians. These prints were painstakingly pasted into family albums and pored over during the dark nights of winter, rekindling precious memories of summer excursions. Frith's studio was soon supplying retail shops all over the country, and by 1890 F Frith & Co had become the greatest specialist photographic publishing company in the world, with over 2,000 sales outlets, and pioneered the picture postcard.

FRANCIS FRITH'S LEGACY

Francis Frith had died in 1898 at his villa in Cannes, his great project still growing. By 1970 the archive he created contained over a third of a million pictures showing 7,000 British towns and villages.

Frith's legacy to us today is of immense significance and value, for the magnificent archive of evocative photographs he created provides a unique record of change in the cities, towns and villages throughout Britain over a century and more. Frith and his fellow studio photographers revisited locations many times down the years to update their views, compiling for us an enthralling and colourful pageant of British life and character.

We are fortunate that Frith was dedicated to recording the minutiae of everyday life. For it is this sheer wealth of visual data, the painstaking chronicle of changes in dress, transport, street layouts, buildings, housing and landscape that captivates us so much today, offering us a powerful link with the past and with the lives of our ancestors.

Computers have now made it possible for Frith's many thousands of images to be accessed almost instantly. The archive offers every one of us an opportunity to examine the places where we and our families have lived and worked down the years. Its images, depicting our shared past, are now bringing pleasure and enlightenment to millions around the world a century and more after his death.

For further information visit: www.francisfrith.com

INTERIOR DECORATION

Frith's photographs can be seen framed and as giant wall murals in thousands of pubs, restaurants, hotels, banks, retail stores and other public buildings throughout Britain. These provide interesting and attractive décor, generating strong local interest and acting as a powerful reminder of gentler days in our increasingly busy and frenetic world.

FRITH PRODUCTS

All Frith photographs are available as prints and posters in a variety of different sizes and styles. In the UK we also offer a range of other gift and stationery products illustrated with Frith photographs, although many of these are not available for delivery outside the UK – see our web site for more information on the products available for delivery in your country.

THE INTERNET

Over 100,000 photographs of Britain can be viewed and purchased on the Frith web site. The web site also includes memories and reminiscences contributed by our customers, who have personal knowledge of localities and of the people and properties depicted in Frith photographs. If you wish to learn more about a specific town or village you may find these reminiscences fascinating to browse. Why not add your own comments if you think they would be of interest to others? See **www.francisfrith.com**

PLEASE HELP US BRING FRITH'S PHOTOGRAPHS TO LIFE

Our authors do their best to recount the history of the places they write about. They give insights into how particular towns and villages developed, they describe the architecture of streets and buildings, and they discuss the lives of famous people who lived there. But however knowledgeable our authors are, the story they tell is necessarily incomplete.

Frith's photographs are so much more than plain historical documents. They are living proofs of the flow of human life down the generations. They show real people at real moments in history; and each of those people is the son or daughter of someone, the brother or sister, aunt or uncle, grandfather or grandmother of someone else. All of them lived, worked and played in the streets depicted in Frith's photographs.

We would be grateful if you would give us your insights into the places shown in our photographs: the streets and buildings, the shops, businesses and industries. Post your memories of life in those streets on the Frith website: what it was like growing up there, who ran the local shop and what shopping was like years ago; if your workplace is shown tell us about your working day and what the building is used for now. Read other visitors' memories and reconnect with your shared local history and heritage. With your help more and more Frith photographs can be brought to life, and vital memories preserved for posterity, and for the benefit of historians in the future.

Wherever possible, we will try to include some of your comments in future editions of our books. Moreover, if you spot errors in dates, titles or other facts, please let us know, because our archive records are not always completely accurate—they rely on 140 years of human endeavour and hand-compiled records. You can email us using the contact form on the website.

Thank you!

For further information, trade, or author enquiries
please contact us at the address below:

**The Francis Frith Collection, Frith's Barn, Teffont,
Salisbury, Wiltshire, England SP3 5QP.**
Tel: +44 (0)1722 716 376 Fax: +44 (0)1722 716 881
e-mail: sales@francisfrith.co.uk **www.francisfrith.com**